Dear Customer

Thank You, for purchasing this book.

When creating these journals it has been our desire to help families share the small things that are so important in creating lifelong family memories. As well we hope that these journals will last and become part of your family history for you, your children and your children's children. Nothing is sadder than looking back at your parents', grand parents' or great-grandparents' lives and realize that you don't know their story.

So please use these journals and document your experiences and feeling, so that when you look back, or your decedents look back, this part of your story will be there for you and for them to enjoy.

Authors

P.S. We pledge that 50% of the author's royalties from the sale of these books will be donated directly to Veteran's Organizations.

This Book Belongs To:

_____

Waiting for my _____:

_____

Who is Deployed to

_____

20____

Date:

Something awesome that I did today…….

_____

_____

_____

_____

_____

_____

_____

_____

_____

_____

_____

_____

_____

I drew a Picture for you today……

Date:

Something awesome that I did today.......

_____

_____

_____

_____

_____

_____

_____

_____

_____

_____

_____

_____

I drew a Picture for you today......

Date:

Something awesome that I did today.......

_____

_____

_____

_____

_____

_____

_____

_____

_____

_____

_____

_____

I drew a Picture for you today......

Date:

Something awesome that I did today…….

_____

_____

_____

_____

_____

_____

_____

_____

_____

_____

_____

_____

I drew a Picture for you today……

Date:

Something awesome that I did today.......

_____

_____

_____

_____

_____

_____

_____

_____

_____

_____

_____

_____

I drew a Picture for you today......

Date:

Something awesome that I did today.......

_____

_____

_____

_____

_____

_____

_____

_____

_____

_____

_____

_____

I drew a Picture for you today......

Date:

Something awesome that I did today.......

_____

_____

_____

_____

_____

_____

_____

_____

_____

_____

_____

_____

I drew a Picture for you today......

Date:

Something awesome that I did today…….

_____

_____

_____

_____

_____

_____

_____

_____

_____

_____

_____

I drew a Picture for you today……

Date:

Something awesome that I did today.......

_____

_____

_____

_____

_____

_____

_____

_____

_____

_____

_____

I drew a Picture for you today......

Date:

Something awesome that I did today…….

I drew a Picture for you today……

Date:

Something awesome that I did today.......

_____

_____

_____

_____

_____

_____

_____

_____

_____

_____

_____

_____

I drew a Picture for you today......

Date:

Something awesome that I did today.......

_____

_____

_____

_____

_____

_____

_____

_____

_____

_____

_____

_____

I drew a Picture for you today......

Date:

Something awesome that I did today…….

_____

_____

_____

_____

_____

_____

_____

_____

_____

_____

_____

_____

I drew a Picture for you today……

Date:

Something awesome that I did today.......

_____

_____

_____

_____

_____

_____

_____

_____

_____

_____

_____

_____

_____

I drew a Picture for you today......

Date:

Something awesome that I did today.......

_____

_____

_____

_____

_____

_____

_____

_____

_____

_____

_____

_____

I drew a Picture for you today......

Something awesome that I did today…….

_____

_____

_____

_____

_____

_____

_____

_____

_____

_____

_____

_____

I drew a Picture for you today……

Date:

Something awesome that I did today.......

I drew a Picture for you today......

Date:

Something awesome that I did today.......

_____

_____

_____

_____

_____

_____

_____

_____

_____

_____

_____

_____

I drew a Picture for you today......

Date:

Something awesome that I did today.......

I drew a Picture for you today......

Date:

Something awesome that I did today.......

_____

_____

_____

_____

_____

_____

_____

_____

_____

_____

_____

_____

I drew a Picture for you today......

Date:

Something awesome that I did today.......

_____

_____

_____

_____

_____

_____

_____

_____

_____

_____

_____

_____

_____

I drew a Picture for you today......

Date:

Something awesome that I did today.......

_____

_____

_____

_____

_____

_____

_____

_____

_____

_____

_____

I drew a Picture for you today......

Date:

Something awesome that I did today.......

_____

_____

_____

_____

_____

_____

_____

_____

_____

_____

_____

I drew a Picture for you today......

Date:

Something awesome that I did today…….

_____

_____

_____

_____

_____

_____

_____

_____

_____

_____

_____

_____

I drew a Picture for you today……

Date:

Something awesome that I did today.......

_____

_____

_____

_____

_____

_____

_____

_____

_____

_____

_____

I drew a Picture for you today......

Date:

Something awesome that I did today…….

_____

_____
_____
_____
_____
_____
_____
_____
_____
_____
_____
_____
_____

I drew a Picture for you today……

Date:

Something awesome that I did today.......

_____

_____

_____

_____

_____

_____

_____

_____

_____

_____

_____

_____

I drew a Picture for you today......

Date:

Something awesome that I did today.......

_____

_____

_____

_____

_____

_____

_____

_____

_____

_____

_____

I drew a Picture for you today......

Date:

Something awesome that I did today.......

_____

_____

_____

_____

_____

_____

_____

_____

_____

_____

_____

_____

I drew a Picture for you today......

Date:

Something awesome that I did today.......

_____

_____

_____

_____

_____

_____

_____

_____

_____

_____

_____

I drew a Picture for you today......

Date:

Something awesome that I did today.......

_____

_____

_____

_____

_____

_____

_____

_____

_____

_____

_____

I drew a Picture for you today......

Date:

Something awesome that I did today.......

I drew a Picture for you today......

Date:

Something awesome that I did today.......

_____

_____

_____

_____

_____

_____

_____

_____

_____

_____

_____

_____

I drew a Picture for you today......

Date:

Something awesome that I did today…….

_____

_____

_____

_____

_____

_____

_____

_____

_____

_____

_____

I drew a Picture for you today……

Date:

Something awesome that I did today…….

I drew a Picture for you today……

Date:

Something awesome that I did today.......

_____

_____

_____

_____

_____

_____

_____

_____

_____

_____

_____

_____

I drew a Picture for you today......

Date:

Something awesome that I did today.......

I drew a Picture for you today......

Date:

Something awesome that I did today.......

_____

_____

_____

_____

_____

_____

_____

_____

_____

_____

_____

_____

I drew a Picture for you today......

Date:

Something awesome that I did today…….

_____

_____

_____

_____

_____

_____

_____

_____

_____

_____

_____

I drew a Picture for you today……

Date:

Something awesome that I did today…….

_____

_____

_____

_____

_____

_____

_____

_____

_____

_____

_____

I drew a Picture for you today…...

Date:

Something awesome that I did today…….

_____

_____

_____

_____

_____

_____

_____

_____

_____

_____

_____

I drew a Picture for you today…...

Date:

Something awesome that I did today…….

_____

_____

_____

_____

_____

_____

_____

_____

_____

_____

_____

_____

I drew a Picture for you today…...

Date:

Something awesome that I did today.......

_____

_____

_____

_____

_____

_____

_____

_____

_____

_____

_____

_____

_____

I drew a Picture for you today......

Date:

Something awesome that I did today…….

_____

_____

_____

_____

_____

_____

_____

_____

_____

_____

_____

I drew a Picture for you today…...

Date:

Something awesome that I did today.......

_____

_____

_____

_____

_____

_____

_____

_____

_____

_____

_____

_____

I drew a Picture for you today......

Date:

Something awesome that I did today…….

_____

_____

_____

_____

_____

_____

_____

_____

_____

_____

_____

_____

I drew a Picture for you today……

Date:

Something awesome that I did today.......

_____

_____

_____

_____

_____

_____

_____

_____

_____

_____

_____

_____

I drew a Picture for you today......

Date:

Something awesome that I did today…….

_____

_____

_____

_____

_____

_____

_____

_____

_____

_____

_____

_____

I drew a Picture for you today……

Date:

Something awesome that I did today.......

I drew a Picture for you today......

Date:

Something awesome that I did today.......

_____

_____

_____

_____

_____

_____

_____

_____

_____

_____

_____

_____

I drew a Picture for you today......

Date:

Something awesome that I did today…….

_____

_____

_____

_____

_____

_____

_____

_____

_____

_____

_____

_____

I drew a Picture for you today……

Date:

Something awesome that I did today…….

_____

_____

_____

_____

_____

_____

_____

_____

_____

_____

_____

_____

I drew a Picture for you today…...

Date:

Something awesome that I did today…….

_____

_____

_____

_____

_____

_____

_____

_____

_____

_____

_____

_____

I drew a Picture for you today……

Date:

Something awesome that I did today…….

_____

_____

_____

_____

_____

_____

_____

_____

_____

_____

_____

I drew a Picture for you today…...

Date:

Something awesome that I did today.......

I drew a Picture for you today......

Date:

Something awesome that I did today…….

_____

_____

_____

_____

_____

_____

_____

_____

_____

_____

_____

_____

_____

I drew a Picture for you today…...

Date:

Something awesome that I did today.......

_____

_____

_____

_____

_____

_____

_____

_____

_____

_____

_____

I drew a Picture for you today......

Date:

Something awesome that I did today.......

_____

_____

_____

_____

_____

_____

_____

_____

_____

_____

_____

I drew a Picture for you today......

Date:

Something awesome that I did today.......

I drew a Picture for you today......

Date:

Something awesome that I did today.......

_____

_____

_____

_____

_____

_____

_____

_____

_____

_____

_____

I drew a Picture for you today......

Date:

Something awesome that I did today…….

_____

_____

_____

_____

_____

_____

_____

_____

_____

_____

_____

_____

_____

I drew a Picture for you today……

Date:

Something awesome that I did today…….

_____

_____

_____

_____

_____

_____

_____

_____

_____

_____

_____

_____

_____

I drew a Picture for you today…...

Date:

Something awesome that I did today…….

_____

_____

_____

_____

_____

_____

_____

_____

_____

_____

_____

_____

_____

I drew a Picture for you today…...

Date:

Something awesome that I did today.......

_____

_____

_____

_____

_____

_____

_____

_____

_____

_____

_____

_____

I drew a Picture for you today......

Date:

Something awesome that I did today…….

_____

_____

_____

_____

_____

_____

_____

_____

_____

_____

_____

_____

I drew a Picture for you today……

Date:

Something awesome that I did today.......

I drew a Picture for you today......

Date:

Something awesome that I did today…….

_____

_____

_____

_____

_____

_____

_____

_____

_____

_____

_____

_____

I drew a Picture for you today……

Date:

Something awesome that I did today.......

_____

_____

_____

_____

_____

_____

_____

_____

_____

_____

_____

I drew a Picture for you today......

Date:

Something awesome that I did today.......

_____

_____

_____

_____

_____

_____

_____

_____

_____

_____

_____

_____

I drew a Picture for you today......

Date:

Something awesome that I did today.......

_____

_____

_____

_____

_____

_____

_____

_____

_____

_____

_____

_____

I drew a Picture for you today......

Date:

Something awesome that I did today.......

_____

_____

_____

_____

_____

_____

_____

_____

_____

_____

_____

_____

I drew a Picture for you today......

Date:

Something awesome that I did today.......

I drew a Picture for you today......

Date:

Something awesome that I did today.......

_____

_____

_____

_____

_____

_____

_____

_____

_____

_____

_____

I drew a Picture for you today......

Date:

Something awesome that I did today.......

_____

_____

_____

_____

_____

_____

_____

_____

_____

_____

_____

_____

I drew a Picture for you today......

Date:

Something awesome that I did today.......

I drew a Picture for you today......

Date:

Something awesome that I did today.......

_____

_____

_____

_____

_____

_____

_____

_____

_____

_____

_____

_____

I drew a Picture for you today......

Date:

Something awesome that I did today…….

_____

_____

_____

_____

_____

_____

_____

_____

_____

_____

_____

_____

I drew a Picture for you today……

Date:

Something awesome that I did today.......

I drew a Picture for you today......

Date:

Something awesome that I did today.......

_____

_____

_____

_____

_____

_____

_____

_____

_____

_____

_____

_____

I drew a Picture for you today......

Date:

Something awesome that I did today.......

_____

_____

_____

_____

_____

_____

_____

_____

_____

_____

_____

_____

I drew a Picture for you today......

Date:

Something awesome that I did today.......

_____

_____

_____

_____

_____

_____

_____

_____

_____

_____

_____

_____

_____

I drew a Picture for you today......

Date:

Something awesome that I did today…….

_____

_____

_____

_____

_____

_____

_____

_____

_____

_____

_____

_____

_____

I drew a Picture for you today……

Date:

Something awesome that I did today…….

I drew a Picture for you today……

Date:

Something awesome that I did today.......

I drew a Picture for you today......

Date:

Something awesome that I did today.......

_____

_____

_____

_____

_____

_____

_____

_____

_____

_____

_____

_____

_____

I drew a Picture for you today......

Date:

Something awesome that I did today.......

_____

_____

_____

_____

_____

_____

_____

_____

_____

_____

_____

_____

I drew a Picture for you today......

Date:

Something awesome that I did today.......

_____

_____

_____

_____

_____

_____

_____

_____

_____

_____

_____

_____

I drew a Picture for you today......

Date:

Something awesome that I did today.......

_____

_____

_____

_____

_____

_____

_____

_____

_____

_____

_____

I drew a Picture for you today......

Date:

Something awesome that I did today.......

_____

_____

_____

_____

_____

_____

_____

_____

_____

_____

_____

_____

I drew a Picture for you today......

Date:

Something awesome that I did today.......

_____

_____

_____

_____

_____

_____

_____

_____

_____

_____

_____

_____

I drew a Picture for you today......

Date:

Something awesome that I did today.......

_____

_____

_____

_____

_____

_____

_____

_____

_____

_____

_____

_____

_____

I drew a Picture for you today......

Date:

Something awesome that I did today.......

_____

_____

_____

_____

_____

_____

_____

_____

_____

_____

_____

I drew a Picture for you today......

Date:

Something awesome that I did today.......

_____

_____

_____

_____

_____

_____

_____

_____

_____

_____

_____

_____

I drew a Picture for you today......

Date:

Something awesome that I did today…….

_____

_____

_____

_____

_____

_____

_____

_____

_____

_____

_____

_____

I drew a Picture for you today…...

Date:

Something awesome that I did today.......

_____

_____

_____

_____

_____

_____

_____

_____

_____

_____

_____

I drew a Picture for you today......

Date:

Something awesome that I did today.......

_____

_____

_____

_____

_____

_____

_____

_____

_____

_____

_____

_____

I drew a Picture for you today......

Date:

Something awesome that I did today.......

_____

_____

_____

_____

_____

_____

_____

_____

_____

_____

_____

_____

_____

_____

I drew a Picture for you today......

Date:

Something awesome that I did today.......

_____

_____

_____

_____

_____

_____

_____

_____

_____

_____

_____

_____

_____

I drew a Picture for you today......

Date:

Something awesome that I did today…….

_____

_____

_____

_____

_____

_____

_____

_____

_____

_____

_____

_____

I drew a Picture for you today……

Date:

Something awesome that I did today.......

_____

_____

_____

_____

_____

_____

_____

_____

_____

_____

_____

_____

I drew a Picture for you today......

Date:

Something awesome that I did today.......

_____

_____

_____

_____

_____

_____

_____

_____

_____

_____

_____

_____

_____

I drew a Picture for you today......

Date:

Something awesome that I did today…….

_____

_____

_____

_____

_____

_____

_____

_____

_____

_____

_____

_____

I drew a Picture for you today……

Date:

Something awesome that I did today.......

_____

_____

_____

_____

_____

_____

_____

_____

_____

_____

_____

_____

I drew a Picture for you today......

Date:

Something awesome that I did today…….

_____

_____

_____

_____

_____

_____

_____

_____

_____

_____

_____

_____

I drew a Picture for you today……

Date:

Something awesome that I did today…….

_____

_____

_____

_____

_____

_____

_____

_____

_____

_____

_____

_____

_____

I drew a Picture for you today……

Date:

Something awesome that I did today.......

_____

_____

_____

_____

_____

_____

_____

_____

_____

_____

_____

_____

I drew a Picture for you today......

Date:

Something awesome that I did today…….

_____

_____

_____

_____

_____

_____

_____

_____

_____

_____

_____

_____

I drew a Picture for you today……

Date:

Something awesome that I did today.......

_____

_____

_____

_____

_____

_____

_____

_____

_____

_____

_____

_____

I drew a Picture for you today......

Date:

Something awesome that I did today.......

_____

_____

_____

_____

_____

_____

_____

_____

_____

_____

_____

_____

I drew a Picture for you today......

Date:

Something awesome that I did today.......

_____

_____

_____

_____

_____

_____

_____

_____

_____

_____

_____

_____

I drew a Picture for you today......

Date:

Something awesome that I did today.......

_____

_____

_____

_____

_____

_____

_____

_____

_____

_____

_____

_____

_____

I drew a Picture for you today......

Date:

Something awesome that I did today.......

_____

_____

_____

_____

_____

_____

_____

_____

_____

_____

_____

_____

I drew a Picture for you today......

Date:

Something awesome that I did today.......

_____

_____

_____

_____

_____

_____

_____

_____

_____

_____

_____

_____

I drew a Picture for you today......

Date:

Something awesome that I did today…….

I drew a Picture for you today…...

Date:

Something awesome that I did today…….

_____

_____

_____

_____

_____

_____

_____

_____

_____

_____

_____

_____

_____

I drew a Picture for you today……

Date:

Something awesome that I did today…….

_____

_____

_____

_____

_____

_____

_____

_____

_____

_____

_____

_____

_____

I drew a Picture for you today…...

Date:

Something awesome that I did today…….

_____

_____

_____

_____

_____

_____

_____

_____

_____

_____

_____

_____

_____

I drew a Picture for you today……

Date:

Something awesome that I did today.......

_____

_____

_____

_____

_____

_____

_____

_____

_____

_____

_____

_____

_____

I drew a Picture for you today......

Date:

Something awesome that I did today.......

_____

_____

_____

_____

_____

_____

_____

_____

_____

_____

_____

_____

I drew a Picture for you today......

Date:

Something awesome that I did today…….

_____

_____

_____

_____

_____

_____

_____

_____

_____

_____

_____

_____

_____

I drew a Picture for you today……

Made in the USA
Las Vegas, NV
07 December 2021

36348268R00068